Intrinsic
Shift

SHIFTING AND WINNING IN LIFE

Intrinsic
Shift

SHIFTING AND WINNING IN LIFE

by

Visionary
Tonia Askins

and

Life Shifter
Tasha Huston

Intrinsic Shift

ISBN_13: 978-0-9910648-2-3

LCCN: 2017918399

Cultivate Press is an imprint of Tonia Askins International LLC.

3001 Ormond Blvd. Ste. F-7
Destrehan, LA 70047
1-866-553-8746
www.toniaaskins.com

Printed in the United States of America

Contents

.
.
.
.
.

Foreword

One morning while I was driving I heard the concept of Intrinsic Shift and was so excited I couldn't pull into the parking
lot fast enough. Once I did park, I realized I didn't have the
time to focus on such a powerful message since I had just
committed to a new position that required dedicated time and
energy. I began to ponder. Who could I trust with such a
powerful message?

Immediately I thought of Tasha and knew she was the
person I could trust with the message of Intrinsic Shift. We
had met a year or so prior, but the spiritual love and connec-
tion was instant. She was someone I knew I could trust and we
always joked that one day we would work on something together, but we didn't know what that project would be.

Knowing the message was full of life and purpose and
would be a game changer for many, my heart was settled after
I reached out to Tasha and she accepted without hesitation.

Once she started writing and sending chapters I was
humbled with gratitude and eagerly awaited the next chapter.

My instructions were to write until you know you're done. The powerful, shifting instructions and insight pouring out of her indeed gave life to the message I received from on High.

The very essence of life is shifting. Many starting inwardly and are very uncomfortable. The key points Tasha developed within this book help you shift gracefully, regardless of the circumstances and pain points you may have to encounter during the shift. I will be forever grateful to God above for such a jewel of knowledge and to Tasha for pouring her heart into this project.

I am completely enamored to present and support the Intrinsic Shift. Enjoy this beautiful message of life, vision, grace and triumph. Peace and Blessings.

Tonia

INTRODUCTION

"You are the sum total of your choices."

—WAYNE DYER

WAS sitting down after mediation one day and this quote hit me like a ton of bricks. As I thought back on my life and took a stroll down memory lane, there was so much I wish I had done differently, a handful of things I didn't regret, and a bucket list full of things yet to pursue. When I looked at this quote that day, I was amazed at how true it had been. In every area of my life, I saw with a different perspective how choice A had led to choice B and so forth. By the end of my relaxation time I was eager to make sure the rest of my life would be the best of my life. I set out to change. Little by little my daily habits begin to look like the visualizations I had for my future. This symphony of changes was orchestrated by one thought:

If I am the sum total of my choices, why had I not made the best possible decisions when it came to finances, education, car buying, food selections, or love? When I first looked at the sum of my life, I was anything but enthused. I was angry. I should have done more. I should have prepared more. I should have said more. Then I thought again. Why had I not done any of those things? The truth is that fear had been a part of my life. Somewhere between friend and enemy was my relationship with it. Until one day I did something in spite of my fear. The situation called for a change and I stood up in the middle of my life answering that call. Many of you reading this are in that place right now. The place where you're not sure what to do but you know you have to do something. There is an internal struggle taking place that has caused you to re-evaluate what you are doing, what you are giving, and you are frantically searching for balance. That struggle is a "shift."

Dictionary.com defines shift as:

1. *To put (something) aside and replace it by another*
2. *To transfer from one place, position, person, etc.*
3. *To move from one direction to another*
4. *To get along by indirect methods*

To shift means to decide that something better is in store for you and to go after it with all your might until you receive it. Shifting is nothing more than a decision followed by perpetual action. It is a repositioning of yourself to catch the blessings in your life. Shifting happens in stages. It must first occur in your mind before it can occur in your feet.

Take for instance a New Year's resolution. On January 1st, I'm sure that just like the rest of us you made a promise to yourself to do something different this year. Maybe it was losing weight or to spend more time with your family. Whatever it is or was, it required a change in your mindset to create it. You made the resolution based on a desire to change. That's great and I'm happy for you. Here we are halfway through the year. Can you remember the resolution? How much progress have you made towards achieving it? You chose to make the resolution. You also chose to follow through or not. Shifting is a choice as well. Sometimes it's painful and you can't see your way thru it. Other times it's remarkable and you wish you had done it sooner. More often than not it's somewhere between painful and remarkable. However it is always bearable. In this book, we will explore the shifting process and get you ready for the best version of you so that when you find yourself in a still, quiet place strolling down memory lane you will have a smile on your face in awe of what you did when you decided to embrace your shift. Going with the flow of things is only as good as the current you ride to get to them.

Chapter One

Respecting the Shift

"The opportunity to experience yourself differently is always available."

—**Yongey Mingyur Rinpoche**

I COULDN'T hear my own thoughts above the internal shouting I was experiencing. What had I done? How was this ok? What would happen to us?

There was a moment in my life that took an insane amount of courage. A time where I second guessed my second guess. I know there are some of you reading this right now and you have found yourself in that same space. The place of uncertainty. The place where life has you by the throat and you are struggling to breathe. I know that there have been times before this one where you have felt a spiritual culmination to be obedient to something deep within you but you just don't know what to do. You feel stuck. You feel uncertain and you might even feel afraid. It's ok. Embrace those feelings. The only constant thing on this side of heaven is change. It is impossible to experience growth on the level that has been purposed to you by remaining where you are. To do so would be resisting your shift which is to be out of alignment with your true self, your purpose, and is displeasing to your creator. You must respect the shift. When you are in a shift, it's uncomfortable. There are no rules. There is no guide on what to do next. Shifting demands that you trust in that deep reservoir of intuition within to pull out of you what is necessary during this season of your life.

To respect something is to have reverence for it. Think about that for a moment. When you are respecting something or someone, you ensure that you never say or do something that would be harmful to them right? You protect the very thing that you respect. In showing reverence for the shift, you are saying to yourself and others that something within is demanding an outward expression different from the one previously displayed.

Take for example the check engine light in a car. When it comes on, most people get a bit panicky and immediately address the situation. However, there are others who don't give much thought to it until it begins to manifest itself in such a way that it will no longer be ignored. It demands that you pay attention to it or the consequences will be costly. When handling a shift, there are two things that can be done. Just like that check engine light, you can address it immediately or you can ignore it and pay for it later. Each choice has a different response. Immediate action results in a less costly outcome.

Delayed action results in damaging consequences. If this is the case and my illustration proves to be correct, why then do we neglect to move when asked to do so? What is it about shifting, changing, newness that paralyzes our purpose? Why does change scare us?

The answer is fear. **Fear has the potential to be a change agent and a deterrent simultaneously.** Think back to a moment where you were truly desperately afraid. I'm certain that as your thoughts bring you back, your body has just sent you a not-so-friendly reminder of that incident in the form of a cringe, flinch, closed eyes, etc. Our minds are magnificent. They have the ability to allow us to still feel the effects of a situation long after it has passed. It is in our moments of fear that we must push through. You are only afraid of what you have yet to conquer. If you knew you would win I'm sure that your level of fear would decrease tremendously. **We were not designed to be afraid.** You want me to prove it? In the bible there are countless scriptures that simply state "Do not be afraid." The reason I believe it is mentioned over and over is that being afraid stops us from growing and that was never the intention of our God. Everything He created He created with the ability to grow exponentially. He intended for us to produce and prosper in every area of our lives.

When I think about shifting it is impossible for me to do so without acknowledging the greatness of a butterfly. It amazes me that what started as an egg, turns into a caterpillar, and enters into a period of chrysalis has the ability to transform into a beautiful butterfly. The butterfly goes through four stages of life. Each stage is coupled with its own degree of obstacles and growing pains, but it is only at the end of each stage that we see a physical sign of growth. Every stage of your life has a measure of time attached to it. If it takes longer than expected, it is due, in part, to our natural affinity to stay where we are not meant to for far longer than was intended. In Deuteronomy 1:6-7, we find the Israelites at Mount Sinai. The word says, *"You have stayed at this mountain long enough. It is time to break camp and move on."* Often times we stay in one spot doing the same thing looking for a change in results. I believe it was Einstein who defined this as insanity. My question to you as you read this book is if the butterfly goes through all of this and still ends up victoriously beautiful what makes you think you can remain the same? Aren't you more capable than a butterfly? When you shift, you should do so with the notion that this shift is necessary and this shift will bring you deeper into your purpose.

Respecting the shift is just as important as the shift itself.

Chapter Two

Shifting Gracefully

Don't let your fear of
what could happen
make nothing happen.

HOW many times in your life do you think you missed out on an opportunity you know for sure was meant for you? As I pose this question to you I do so to myself also. I wonder how many times a miracle was before me and I didn't recognize it. How many times has God answered my prayer and I didn't know it because I refused to look at it in that light? We think that miracles come in these beautiful amazing packages wrapped in gold with a huge "M" stamped to the side of it. That's just not so.

A miracle is a wondrous marvel. All throughout the bible we see miracles take place from Genesis to Revelation. It is in those unexplainable times that the most compassionate act of

God took place. In your life there will be miracles. I like to call miracles God-winks that remind us of his goodness. Miracles are heavenly shifts that he sends down and leaves to us to receive. It is his way of saying I see you, I see your need, and I have the solution.

While fear may paralyze a shift, there is something else that stops us from shifting and that something is time. We as humans believe that we have this infinite amount of time to complete, to do, to act, to figure out. The truth is that we don't have time. Time has us. We are the captives of time. We wear watches to keep up with how much of our day has passed. We make schedules, follow routines, and race clocks to ensure we get everything we have on these massive to-do lists accomplished. Shifting takes time but it doesn't have to take all of it.

Something happens when we shift. **Shifting allows us to free up time previously allocated to other areas of our life and position it to be perfectly placed within our intended purpose.** How would you feel if you had more time to do what you really felt led to do? Take for instance the person reading this that has always wanted to start a business, go back to school, follow their creative dreams, open a restaurant or be the co-founder of a non-profit organization. The first thing that stops you is time and the second thing would be money. You never have time for this or that but you have plenty of time to sit on social media sites posting, liking, and sharing. Time is one of the most precious commodities gifted to mankind. Just think God said in Ecclesiastes 3:1 *to everything there is a season and a time to every purpose under the heaven.*

He never mentions how much time but it is available to us. Why then, if something has been given to us so freely, do we waste it so carelessly? No one knows when their time is up so wouldn't it be useful to do something amazing with the time you do have? Having this in mind, you should never remain stuck in a place when shifting is available. You don't have time for that.

Change is hard but it is also necessary. You must take responsibility for the shifts that have come to you and adjust accordingly. You must shift from being to doing. Don't just be the one with a dream. Be the one **making** their dream come true. Don't just be the one living from paycheck to paycheck. Be the one **making** small investments into a savings account. Trust the internal compass within you so much that even if you're afraid to make the jump leap anyway. You are the product of a God that **CAN NOT fail.** The only way to ensure failure is to do nothing in the first place. Trust the shift. When something big happens in your life and it requires a shift don't play with it. Any type of shift requires courage but it cannot be executed properly without internal wisdom. Pray about it. This is how you can tell if you are experiencing a shift:

- ❀ When you find yourself in a place where shifting is a requirement
- ❀ When you are between moving forward or looking back
- ❀ When it seems like life is kicking your butt one too many times and you can't catch a break
- ❀ When everyone around you says something is wrong with what you believe to be normal

- When other factors such as stress, anxiety or depression seep into your life suddenly or resurface a shift is inevitable

- When your intuition kicks into overdrive anytime you think about the idea of doing something greater than what you are currently doing.

To do something with grace means to do something with ease. How many of you can relate that when a shift hits your life it is anything but graceful? I cannot recount the many times I found myself face to face with a new version of myself. The new version looked amazing on the outside but she had been broken, bruised, misguided, and afraid prior to what you see now. The same goes for you. There will come a time in your life where you must shift with grace even when it hurts to do so. Think back to a life moment you had where you remember being utterly confused and downright foolish. Now, I want you to smile. Had you not been foolish then, your wisdom wouldn't be as important to you as it is now. I have to be honest with you, shifting hurts. When it's worth it, it will take the most out of you. That's what growth does. Remember those bean plants you did in school as a kid. Your teacher usually put it in a clear plastic 8 oz. cup and told you to water it and put it in the sun. You watched it grow. You were excited about every step of the process probably driving your parents crazy with the daily updates. Even when you couldn't see it, went to school, or fell asleep the plant kept growing. Then one day something magical happens. You find yourself searching for a larger container for your NEW plant. Can I tell you what happened? This plant started as a seed. Then, in the right environment and under the correct conditions it was allowed to flourish. However, at its peak, it had to shift to a larger container for it had outgrown its first home. Some of you reading this right now are in a season of plucking and pruning. You have found yourself in overflow. You have outgrown your current situation and are looking for a new place to thrive. There is absolutely nothing wrong with that. That's what seeds are supposed to do. They, much like a baby in the womb, stretch the soil to make room for their growth. They give way to life. Life does not stop because we won't shift. In fact it will get so uncomfortable in that comfort zone that a shift will literally make you bust at the seams. Take it in stride. Do not begin to stitch a hole that was created to be a tear. Sometimes God will take that hole, that tear in what you thought it was going to look like and use it as a peep hole for where he wants to take you. Pay attention to the areas where there is massive growth and those where there is no growth. These areas are very telling of where a shift needs to occur. When you shift gracefully it is not the absence of pain, issues, worry, or anger. It is what takes place when all hell looks like it broke loose and no one can tell from your response to it.

Chapter Three

Honor the Pause
That Comes with Your Shift

"Even five minutes spent in silence
will nurture & revive
your soul and spirit."

—DOREEN VIRTUE

I CANNOT go one day without meditating. Doing so completely throws my day off track. It came in handy when I lost my dad. I was so angry and so anxious. My mind was a loose cannon to say the least. Meditation was my chosen therapy. When I started out it was a bit of a struggle. I knew how to be quiet however my mind needed more practice than I thought. I watched video after video for techniques and searched for the perfect meditation mantra. The day came where my practice of this ancient art form could be tested. I laid in my bed, played the music, sat the way I had been instructed and waited. I waited for the big "bang" the feeling it would bring. I was hurting and wanted some relief. I waited some more. That fifteen minutes felt like an eternity. The chime sounded and there in the middle of my bed I cussed. Out loud. I just spent fifteen minutes of precious sleep time trying to be still and all I felt in that moment was more anxiety. I walked to the bathroom and cussed. Put on my clothes and cussed some more. I was convinced that cussing was the answer and not meditation. I went through that entire day on edge and you guessed it...cussing, A LOT. This went on for a few weeks. When I returned home one evening after a long day at the office all I wanted to do was relax. I tried a bath and it didn't work. I felt an urgency to still my mind, to empty its contents and let myself feel whatever it was I hadn't allowed it to feel before. All out of options I grabbed my bible, my phone, and I sat down with myself. I knew that something had to change. After praying, I laid once more on my bed. I took a deep breath and hit the app on my phone. Twenty minutes later I felt better. I felt relieved, refreshed, and like a weight had been lifted off my shoulders. Twenty minutes of surrendering to the silence. Twenty minutes of letting go, casting cares, giving up what I couldn't control in the first place, and having that real talk with myself, with God. I couldn't get enough of the feeling it gave me so I gradually incorporated it into my daily routine. I thought about how much I enjoyed going to the beach. The salted air, the fresh breeze, and the warm sand in-between my toes make me want to go all the time. My favorite time on the beach is right before sunset. As the birds are flying home and the sun is setting, the sky does this magical thing. It goes from a blanket of baby blue canvas to hues of orange, yellow, and coral intertwining before your very eyes. I sit and watch God's work unfold right there. I sit. I am stilled by his awesomeness, his majestic power. Some of you may be sitting there wondering why in the world I would want to sit still on purpose when I don't have to. No worries I had a similar question. It is within those moments of silence that we are ushered into a deeper realm. **It is in my opinion where we occupy the gap between heaven and earth.** Those minute moments of silence are monumental. It is in these moments that God speaks clearly and directly to us.

Take for instance in Exodus 19:4 where Moses climbs a mountain and then God speaks to him. In this text we don't know how much time has elapsed, though we do know for sure is that it takes more than five minutes to climb a mountain. How many mountains have you had to climb before God would speak to you?

Regardless of your stage in life right now, you are always climbing a mountain. Some of us find ourselves at the bottom looking up and wondering how we will ever get to the top of this enormous monstrosity whose top seems so far away. Many of us are in the middle hanging on for dear life trusting, pulling, pushing, and fighting to get there. There are a few who are at the top and find that when they get there that it feels as though God is not. Believe me he is there. He was there when you started and he will be waiting for you right there when you finish. When we learn how to quiet our mind and our actions before him, he empowers us with the ability to get impossible things done in the earth.

There is a certain pause that happens to us as we shift. It causes us to stop dead in our tracks and take heed to what is or is not occurring. Shifting as we know it is all about change and improvement from moment to moment. Being still is the answer we give to show him we honor his place in our life.

Being still causes two things to happen. First, it allows us to see where we are and where we are headed. Second, it allows us to relinquish control of how we are to get there. For example, let's say we are headed to the museum by bus. We travel to the bus stop and sit. A few minutes pass by and there is no sign of the bus coming. We look up the bus schedule. A few more minutes go by, there's no sign of the bus and we both begin to get a little antsy. We wait some more. Finally the bus arrives. We ride in silence, we wait in silence, and we can only take the designated route assigned to the driver by the dispatcher. On the route we run into traffic, slow moving cyclists, a 3 car pile-up, and we swerve in the nick of time to miss hitting a car. I don't know about you but upon arrival I would be less concerned with how I got there and more grateful that I had arrived safely.

That's what happens when you climb mountains. Some of the surfaces are designed for climbers and some are not. **The trick is to find your footing on every inch of it, find those hand grooves and do whatever it takes to get to the top no matter how many jagged edges you find along the way. Jagged edges are not stops signs, they are mere reminders of progress.** They are moments of stillness for us to gather our might, channel the voice within, and fight our way to the top of that mountain.

Chapter Four

The Shifting Effect

"All great changes are
preceded by chaos."

—DEEPAK CHOPRA

SIDE effects, the results of your body interacting with a medication. They are such awful little things aren't they? The crazy thing about them is that they reach far beyond the prescription bottle. Side effects are also happening all around you. They are these little capsules of uncertainty floating in and out of your life.

For example, let's say you are looking for a job. You have one now and are happy there but you could use more money. The opportunity comes along and you find a job that you would really love to do. It's a perfect fit for you, and it's not too far from your house so it cuts down on your commute. You are ecstatic. While the increase in pay is more than what you expected, the downside is you would now have to work weekends. What do you do? In most cases some would take the job, some would not, and a few others would find a happy medium.

Side effects mimic the interactions we have with ourselves. There is always a cause and effect happening whether it is known or unknown. Shifting causes change and change causes anxiety, restlessness, and lack of control. When your life is experiencing so many changes all at once it can be overwhelming and you may feel that the world is not on your side especially when you take a look around and it appears that everyone else is doing better than you. Can I share a secret? Everyone is doing the same thing you are. Everyone is living and shifting accordingly. What you see is the finished product, not their process. The process of shifting is so intricate and infinite in detail that to understand why you are going through what you are going through you have to go back to the beginning of it all. If you ask me, Adam and Eve sealed our fate after eating that apple. So here we are smack dab in the middle of life without a lifeboat or so it seems.

When you feel like you are drowning look up. **If Jesus can help Peter walk on water surely he can help you fix your finances, fix your family, fix the deeply rooted circumstance that is kicking your butt.** Side effects of life are not meant to paralyze us. They are meant to show us how the domino effect of our daily decisions impact every aspect of our lives.

It is going to be chaotic, it is going to be uncomfortable but trust that it is necessary. You won't be able to sustain the blessing if you are trying to soften the blow. Blessings come after a bit of bruising. Blessings are given every day. They are an outward expression of how the work within is manifesting. All change whether great or small requires a decision. There is something that needs to shift and you know it but we get quite comfortable. We are only able to produce according to our level of comfort. If you are comfortable making $500 a week and you put in no effort to make a dollar more, then $500 a week is your level. However, if there is an innate stirring within you that simply says "What if…" and you follow it, you will see changes start to occur. Not only have your actions shifted but that small mindset modification has shifted your life.

I always thought when I would hear people say "if you want to change your life, change the way you think." What do my thoughts have to do with me wanting to take a trip to Italy? Or what do your thoughts have to do with you wanting to achieve anything in life?

Your thoughts are the holding place for your life. Your life is a direct reflection of your thought patterns. Everything you have right now is due in part to a thought you had. As you look at your life and process those thoughts, I know some of those decisions popping out at you right now weren't the best, the greatest, the nicest, or the smartest. That's ok. What you did only governs who you are if you allow it to. You have the power to change your thoughts. You have the power to change your life. You are one thought away from being the best version of yourself. The trick is not to get caught up in the smoke screen of chaos.

Chaos by definition is: *a state of utter confusion or disorder; lack of organization.*

You know what I like most about chaos? God. Let me explain. In Genesis 1:1, God created the heavens and the earth. In Genesis 1:2, it states that the earth was formless, empty, and filled with darkness. Can you imagine going from day to day in the dark? Imagine trying to get ready for work, completing chores, or getting kids off to school? I want you to imagine your life as it is now and what you would like for it to look like. Now imagine having to do it all in the dark, completely blindfolded, no electricity whatsoever. Would it be as enjoyable as you first imagined it to be? Would you get the same feelings you did when you first closed your eyes?

Darkness is chaotic. Darkness is uncertain and uncomfortable. Darkness is heavy and burdensome. It is only when the light has been switched on that we are flooded with relief. **There is power in light.** Want me to prove it? The very first thing God did after he made the heavens and earth, after he looked upon it and saw all the emptiness was simply state "Let there be light." The illuminating power of light drives out the intent of darkness. If you will notice, everything you use has a light from cars to cellphones. Light is intentional. Light is purposeful. Light brings life into dark situations. If you are experiencing a rather dark time get still, embrace where you are, respect where you are, and then go purposefully into the light for your life.

Chapter Five

The Purpose of a Shift

"You have to believe
no matter what has come against you,
no matter how unfair it was,
things are shifting in your favor."

—Joel Osteen

WHEN I was younger I can remember being in Saturday Science Academy. On Saturdays mama would drop us off and we would explore biology, chemistry, and all things in-between. I was always fascinated by what we learned whether it was the anatomy of a pig, seeing a human autopsy, or dissecting my first frog. It prepared me in so many ways for high school and life that I often find myself reflecting back on my time there. The knowledge gained in that place wasn't put to immediate use, but over the years I have applied it to my life. The definition of purpose according to dictionary.com is:

Purpose: *the reason for which something exists, is done, made, or used; an intended or desired result.*

Purpose always asks "why?" Think about the times you were face to face with a difficult decision, unmovable mountain, or an unfair circumstance. I can almost guarantee you wanted to know "why." Why is this happening to me? Why have they treated me like this? Why didn't I receive that promotion? We spend more time asking why then we do seeking the answer. There is a reason for everything. There is a reason you are who you are, designed the way you are, look the way you do, and are interested in the things that bring you joy. It's all tied to your purpose. Your purpose, like a bridge, is the connecting piece to something far greater than yourself. Your purpose of helping one person indirectly helps thousands of people you may never come in contact with. How awesome is that. Great news right? **The greatest shift of your life will happen just before you find out your true purpose.**

Let me give you an example through the account of Joseph (Gen. 37-45). In the story of Joseph, his brothers are jealous of him and his relationship with their father. They devise a plan to kill him but later decide to sell him into slavery. Thus begins his journey to his purpose. After being sold to an Egyptian, he soon found himself in a position of influence as his master's personal attendant. After being falsely accused of rape, he was placed into prison. He later became the ruler of Egypt serving as second in command to the King of Egypt. During his serving, a famine struck the land. All the surrounding areas ran out of food and had to come to Joseph to receive rations. His brothers, the same brothers who sold him into slavery (starting what appeared to be a downfall was his greatest victory) now needed him.

Joseph's greatest shift started with slavery. I know it sounds weird to say and even crazier to fathom that in order to get him to where he needed to be God orchestrated something so inhumane. Maybe your process won't involve slavery or maybe you have found yourself in the place of uncertainty feeling stuck. One situation after another is threatening to devour you, your peace of mind, your finances, and your family. Be assured that it has purpose. There is purpose in your pain and your struggle. It is not a coincidence that what has happened or what will happen in your life is without purpose. You must remain mindful of this and persevere by pulling from the deep reservoir of faith that you possess. It will not be easy but it will be worth it. I came across a passage from *In Pursuit of Purpose* by Dr. Myles Munroe:

> "God's purposes always prevail. Once God tells you His purpose for your life, relax. He's already told your predestination, so no matter how much pressure comes or how many problems threaten you, they cannot overcome you."

I found this passage to be so gratifying and encouraging. There are times we will be face to face with adversity and all we feel surrounding us is defeat and discouragement. We get so bogged down with worry and solutions that we neglect to acknowledge that it isn't our problem to fix what we are going through in the first place.

The point of "going through" something is to GO THROUGH IT. Not whine or complain about being in it. Let's say for example someone offered you a million dollars to trek through an unknown terrain. I'm sure some of you would need more time to consider it and others would say yes without hesitation. They re-assure you that the terrain has been traveled by many, has some beautiful sights, and in addition to the million dollars they will pay for all of your gear, airfare, etc. You are ecstatic a free trip and the possibility of a million dollars sounds good right? What they neglected to point out was the destination, the scarce access to food you would have, or the countless wild animals you would encounter along the way. Knowledge of the journey before the process defeats the strength you are intended to gain from your progress. That's why it clearly states that the race is not given to the swift but to the one who endures. If your purpose wasn't so important don't you think that everyone would be able to do it? You are the only person that can do what you can do. Someone may be able to mimic your actions but NO ONE can do it quite like you.

Tap into those gifts and desires you have been holding on to the ones no one knows about but you and your source. Unleash them into the world and don't be surprised by the goodness that will follow you when you do. Do not be put off by the magnitudes of your life shifts. Embrace them. Get through them. Enjoy them. Troubles although seemingly endless and gigantic can only be tackled one step at a time. They are also temporary. The duration depends on how long you decide to stay outside of your purpose. It will not only delay your shifts but the shifts of others directly and indirectly connected to you. Your purpose is for others not just you.

Chapter Six

Be Kind to Yourself While Shifting

"Do not speak badly of yourself.
For the warrior within hears
your words and is lessened by them."

—DAVID GEMMELL

AS a child, when you are upset, they instruct you to count to ten. As an adult that gets angry, when you can't figure something out, all anyone can say is "calm down don't worry about it." I often find myself looking back at the younger version of myself. I wonder how often she had to be quiet or how many times she was overlooked by a parent, an adult, a more talented peer. I wonder what I would have told her back then if I would have known everything I know now. There are times in our lives where we step onto a battlefield unprepared to fight. Sure we have all the tools to win. To the naked eye we look like the champion but the appearance of a thing and the reality of it are two different things.

Take for instance the story of Joshua. Joshua was the successor of Moses. Moses was charged with bringing the Israelites into the Promised Land but because of his disobedience that task was taken from him. Joshua picks up where Moses left off. In the beginning, when Joshua is charged with the great task of taking them into the Promised Land, he doubts his ability to do it. He immediately starts telling God all the reasons why picking him is a bad idea. How many times have you been led to complete or asked to do a thing and you did not follow through? You came up with every excuse you could think of or even enlisted the help of others to come up with even more excuses. The quickest way to lose a blessing is to talk yourself out of it. Often times we get discouraged with such tasks. How am I supposed to raise this child alone Lord, I'm not married, how am I supposed to walk this road alone Lord, no one supports this dream you have given me, how am I supposed to start this business have you seen my bank account. There is nowhere in the word where it gives explicit instructions on "how to do something," God is too strategic for that. He simply asks us to do two things: believe and trust. He takes care of the when, what, why, and the way. He took away every excuse he felt the Israelites would come up with to go back to Egypt, a place where they were slaves, held captive mentally and physically, even though it was their home, even though it was the only thing they knew how to do. He moved them. He set them free. When a shift like this happens in your life, a shift where the only option you have in order to continue to grow is to move forward, do this for yourself "GO!" There are over 90 definitions for the word "go" according to dictionary.com. While I won't list them all here are a few:

to move or proceed; to leave a place; to keep or be in motion; to reach or extend

To go does not mean to forget. It simply means that you have stayed where you are and you have outgrown that space. Who we are as people we were never meant to stay stagnant. We are filled with the fiery currents of the Holy Spirit. We are designed intricately with mounds of flexibility. Do you think it is a coincidence that our bodies are composed of 90% water? Water flows. We are to flow from shift to shift with grace but there are moments this doesn't happen so easily. Quiet moments where we spend time in secret places doubting self. In those moments be kind to yourself. Your words have power. Your words have creative power. Everything in your life right now is due in part to the very words you have spoken over it. Some of us have used words to elevate and uplift. Others have used words to demean and denounce. Regardless of the way you used them there is still power in how you choose to use them now.

I have found that being kind takes little effort. It is the simplest daily decision we can make. It is the act of doing for one another as you would like for them to do for you in return. Being kind makes you feel good regardless of how you felt before completing that act. If you don't believe me I dare you to seek out one way to be kind today and see if it doesn't yield an automatic feeling of gratitude. Being kind to others is easier than being kind to yourself. We have been trained to think that thinking of yourself, being nice to yourself is in a way selfish. It is not. If the words you spoke to yourself were unleashed in a room of your closest friends, how would you feel? My mom used to tell my sister and I this saying when we were little. We still use it to this day. She would tell us "don't be ugly." It was her way of ensuring we knew that words hurt people and that hurt people, hurt people. When you have found yourself facing a difficult circumstance and you do not know what to do or what to think the innate response is to talk down to yourself. To embrace what could go wrong instead of focusing on what could go right. Being kind to yourself is the only way you will ever be authentically kind to others. If I talked to people the way I talked to myself sometimes, I wouldn't have many friends. Why then do we even participate in this act? It stems from thinking that we have to have it all figured out. There is this life I have to live or want to live and I must go from A-Z to get there. The truth is we have no more control over our lives than we do the weather. We are all at the mercy of the Father. He's already decided what our lives will be. Speaking life into your life is the best way to ensure success. To ensure that what you say you want, you receive. Be careful with the words you speak. Remember you are the first one to hear them loudly.

Chapter Seven

Drifting vs. Shifting

"Let go or be dragged."

—ZEN PROVERB

*"Sometimes
your only available transportation
is a leap of faith."*

—MARGARET SHEPARD

LATE one Friday after work, I was on my way home except I wasn't ready to go. Trust me, I had millions of things to do once I got there but the car was so peaceful and quiet I wanted to drive a little longer. I just wanted to be for a moment. Eventually, I grew hungry and made my way home. A funny thing happened in between work and home though. I found myself just wandering, no set direction. I drove not worrying about what came next in my life. I was keenly focused on driving, listening to music, and enjoying the idea of not going to work for the next two days. It was blissful. I was able to de-clutter my mind from the past week. It felt amazing. It felt right. Often times we get to a place in life where we forget the beauty and power in existing in the moment because we lead such hurried lives always thinking in terms of "next" never fully enjoying the state of "now."

What is it about now that is so scary to us? Here's what I've learned. Now matters to us only when it suits us. When it fits into our schedule. If it in any way appears to go against something we wanted then we tend to put it off. Take for example what happened to Jonah. Jonah had been given a directive by God. In Jonah 1:2, it's very simple. God spoke asking Jonah to get up and go to Nineveh. Nothing wrong there. Seems simple enough right? However in verse three, Jonah is said to have gotten up and ran in the opposite direction in which he was told to. Can I tell you a secret? I have a bit of Jonah in me. There have been past encounters I have run from even after I was directed to go to a certain place, talk to a certain person, or perform a certain action. The story continues with Jonah running and God telling him again to go to Nineveh. God eventually grows tired of Jonah's disobedience, causes a storm to come against the boat that has him, and his shipmates throw him overboard after casting lots to see who had upset the Gods. They throw Jonah overboard and the sea immediately becomes calm. Jonah is swallowed by a great fish. He spends three days and three nights in the belly of that fish.

After reading this passage, I had a series of thoughts. One of them stuck out to me. Why is it when God says **go** we hesitate even when going is in our best interest? We tense up because we do not know what is on the other side of that go. A wall of uncertainty has manifested itself in our minds and we look at it, dwell on it, and live in it so much so that moving outside of it seems abnormal. Ignoring the shift will not decrease its importance. Ignoring your shift only causes your blessings to be delayed or in some instances derailed. It also causes the blessings of those tied to you to be delayed as well. Let's say for example you have found yourself in a toxic relationship. You want to be out of it but you've been it in so long that this is home, this is normal. You feel something urging you to walk away but your feet can't seem to match the courage your mind has to leave, to disconnect. What if you found out that attached to your leaving was a release of others from similar battles. What if your leaving was the testimony needed to free someone else from bondage. When you are given instructions to go to a place, or talk to a person allow me to encourage you to do so. There are so many people connected to your obedience of one action, whatever that action may be. As we later found out with Jonah, he was sent to deliver a message to the people of Nineveh. An entire Kingdom turned back to God and away from their wicked ways because of one man's obedience to deliver a message. As individuals we have the power to set ENTIRE KINGDOMS free with our obedience. Literally all Jonah did was speak what God told him to say and it was done. What have you been putting off saying? What have you been asked to do but haven't? What are you doing now not next? There is no greater time than now. I need you to stop drifting and start shifting.

To drift means to:

Drift: *a driving movement or force; to be carried along by the force of circumstances; to wander aimlessly; to deviate from a set course*

Deviation from an intended plan can wreak havoc on your life. When you are in tune with the purpose within, your idle time no longer exists. You stop going about life drifting, trying to find your way, trying to figure it all out, and you begin to work on becoming. Regardless of what it looks like around you be encouraged in following the shift taking place within you. The intrinsic shift. That innate knowing that pushes you, forces you out of bed, propels you take one step and then another is the most important thing about you. If you truly knew the ability of the one within you, your doubts would starve themselves to death. Do you know what can happen to you if you continue to wander aimlessly? You will end up on a path where you don't belong, connected to people you were never meant to meet, experiencing things you were not supposed to. You will find yourself on a broken journey. There is nothing worse than being on a path headed nowhere. Misguided direction is not of God. He will never lead you where he is not. If you have found yourself on a journey and things are looking a bit bleak, you can't keep your head up, or everything around you is falling apart, I implore you to take a few steps back. Find out who is leading you. Ask yourself what was it you were asked to do and is what you're doing now preparing you for what's next.

Our lives arc but a reflection of choices made and unmade. We are to be here but for a moment. Do not use your time drifting aimlessly through a life you were designed to live abundantly. That's like having unlimited access to a mansion as your home but choosing to live month to month in a shack instead. You are gifted only one life. Live it on purpose. Do not allow drifting to eliminate the power of shifting.

Chapter Eight

The Unanticipated Blessing
of a Shift

"As much as you want to plan your life,
it has a way of surprising you with
unexpected things that will make you
happier than you originally planned.
That's what you call God's will."

—UNKNOWN

SHIFTS, much like people, come in all shapes and sizes. They can be instant. They can take a while. They can be big or small. They can be good or bad but it will always happen. There is nothing any of us can do to stop the progress of change. It's out of our control. How does something we can't control cause us the most grief? That's simple. As humans we like being in control and when something threatens that control, we lose it. Take for instance coffee. I know there are many of us who are coffee drinkers or tea lovers. We plan our morning around that first cup. If that first cup is good the day will be great however, if anyone tries to talk to you prior to that first cup some of you will be a tad bit cranky right?

Shifts are kind of like that. It's that uncertain, unexpected conversation you don't want to have without having coffee first. A lot of life's shifts come at the most inconvenient time. If only we could schedule shifts and CC Jesus when we are ready for them life would be a lot easier to handle. Shifts don't work like that. Contrary to popular belief they have a way of putting some much needed fire under our butts to get in alignment with what is happening and to do so rather quickly. Shifts come without warning. Have you ever experienced a period in life where it felt as though everything was shifting at once? I mean one thing after another was coming at you and you were close to losing your mind. That's what happened in the book of Job. In one day Job lost his sources of income, his children, his health and his servants. His wife wanted him to curse God. Job goes through a series of internal battles and external battles with his friends. Everyone is trying to convince him to give up on God and give into the anger and resentment he feels towards him. Throughout the entire process the only thing that did not waiver was his faith in God. After some time and recommitting to God, EVERYTHING he lost was restored and then some. He experienced an insurmountable amount of pain and suffering with all that he had lost. When we lose something we believe to be of great value unexpectedly, the natural reaction is to become upset. To grieve it. To act out in rage and to take it out on anyone in our path. Can I share with you the best action step to take regardless of the situation? Pray. The bible says to pray without ceasing. We are to pray constantly. Our prayer does not stop things from happening to us but it allows what has happened or what will happen not to destroy us. **Pain is a catalyst for positioning.** There is always a blessing that comes attached to our pain. It is difficult to see it at first but it is true. When you are aligned properly you are in the best place for receiving what is meant to be yours. You ever had a moment in your life that something unexpected happened to you because you were in the right place at the right time? What is it about an unexpected blessing that reaffirms what we already know? That something greater is at hand. It reminds me of the story of the poor widow and Elisha (2 Kings 4:1-7). Here a woman's husband has died, she has two children, and she cannot afford to pay her bills. She was given a directive to go into her house with as many jars as she could find and to fill them with oil. No matter how many times I read this story it always comes to mind that she used oil. Some of us have found ourselves at this place a time or two. A place of desperation. A place where there appears to be little to no hope. God is trying to get something to us but we look at his method of "oil" with a smirk on our faces. In that place we are trying to figure it out on our own and someone is depending on us to make things better. That someone could be your child, your parents, your significant other, or even yourself. The situation looks bad, really bad and there is so much pressure. This woman. This widowed woman took this man's advice and filled the jars until she had filled each of them. The oil stopped flowing and then she was told to go and sell them to pay off her debts. What if she would have turned her nose up at the prophet's suggestion? What would have become of her and her children or their home? I'm not sure if you have come face to face with a rude creditor but not much about their methods has changed since then. She cried out to this man for help and he gave her the tools for her situation. Her obedience produced the very thing she had asked for. There was an unexpected, unanticipated blessing attached to her obedience.

Some of you reading this right now have been sitting on gifts, talents, books, sermons, TV shows, organizations, businesses, schools, and shelters because you won't shift. I know you had a plan for your life. I also know that the plan you had and the life you live may not be going in the direction that you hoped it would. There is a greater plan for you. The beauty about this plan is that it may not look like what you thought it would but it will bless you in ways you couldn't have imagined for yourself. Shifting is not a letting go of your ideals but an acceptance of what your life is truly meant to be. It is the permission we give ourselves to say "yes." Yes to God's ways and his will. It positions us to get out of our own way and trust that it is working out in our favor.

Chapter Nine

Sifting and Shifting

"Sometimes you get the best light from a burning bridge."

—DON HENLEY

BAKING helps to declutter my mind. It's something about being elbow deep in flour, counter tops decorated with various ingredients, and a warm welcoming oven that has an instant soothing element to it. Perhaps it is the idea of creating something wonderful as the different aromas hit the tip of your nostrils. Then all of a sudden after all the kneading, mixing, and stirring has been done there is the beautiful sound of a "ding" that indicates that it's ready. If only life was as easy as mixing and stirring of ingredients. In essence, I believe it is. The thing that we get all mixed up is trying to add the wrong ingredients and expecting that same luscious life we were promised. It's like false advertisement yet the only one to blame is ourselves. In my most recent trip to the kitchen, the recipe just like countless others before it called for the dry ingredients to be sifted. I remembered from an earlier cooking class what the "sifter" looked like and so I set my sights on finding it amongst the pots and pans. I looked everywhere for that darn thing but it never surfaced. Where is my "sifter?" How am I supposed to make what I believe to be the best cookie on earth without it? The "sifter" is in fact a sieve. It is a wonderful invention really. It allows for the flour or any other dry ingredient to go through a process of removing unwanted, unnecessary, clumps. It is purposed to break up those clumps, separate them from one another and aerate them before being added to the mixture. The overall purpose of a sieve is to ensure that only the best quality of the chosen ingredient be used to make the finished product.

As I sat and thought about that for a moment I was in awe. If a sifter could do that with flour, surely God had even more in store for me. **The process of being sifted takes only a moment but its results are finite.** The flour can never be returned to its original state full of clumps and bumps after being sifted. The same can be said of us as we go into and come out of a shift. There is no way we can remain the same. You may even be asking yourself "why do I have to be sifted?" There are some things in life, more importantly some people that are not meant to go where you are headed next. I know that there are people we wish we could hold onto for dear life but for reasons unknown to us they can't come. This can be devastating but it is the necessary ingredient to your growth.

Imagine you are holding a big, burly tug-of-war type rope

in your hands. You are holding onto one end of it. You are using every ounce of strength to pull it onto your side but it just won't budge. Whatever is on the other end is heavy and stubborn but you don't give up. Until one day you look at your hands. They have become callused, bloody, and unrecognizable. They are racked with pain. The weight of the other side is strong. We cannot begin to grasp within our mindset how heavy it is yet we go day by day carrying it, dragging it, and pulling it. Until all of its heaviness has shown up in a more magnified way in every season of our life. The weight of pain or heartache from 20 years, 10 years, or 5 years. Yet we stand next to our peers, colleagues, family members and friends as if we have it all together when in reality we are ill-fitted pieces of a puzzle we do not have the strength to put together again. They don't know that we lack mental rest, peace, and are literally surviving on bits and pieces of joy. Why? Why are you putting yourself through that? In John 10:10: *The thief's purpose is to steal and kill and destroy. My purpose is to give them a rich and satisfying life.* Holding on to dead weight makes for a heavy load. The reason you have yet to let it go is because you are afraid to face who you will become without it. It is my belief that the number one destroyer of newness is oldness. How will you ever enjoy the fullness of the new life if you are still reaching back, hands clasped tightly around the old one? To enjoy something is to be "in" it joyously.

Let's say you have an event scheduled for a particular day and you have an old friend coming into town at the same time. Which would you choose? I bet many of you would choose to hang out with your old friend and then later decide how important the event was. There is no right or wrong answer here but I want you to pay attention to the reasoning used in your decision. The initial feeling you get from hearing about the possibility of seeing an old friend is the same feeling you should have EVERY DAY OF YOUR LIFE. The possibility of joy should be enough to catapult you into action but if that old friend has nothing new to say to the new you I'm sure you would have chosen the event instead. Step away from the old way and embrace the newness. There is nothing wrong with the way you do things but if you are reading this then the way you are doing them could use a revamp. I want you take a moment and do an internal sifting. Sift through your thoughts, daily routine, life patterns, relationships, choices, and see if there isn't anything or anyone that needs to be "sifted" out of your way so that you can live that full life promised to you. Sifting is not a cutting out. It is cutting away from the thing that has been holding you back.

Some of us have been standing still in the middle of our own lives. It is time to rise up and take that step. Yes, it will be scary. Yes, at first it will be difficult. Yes, you will be met with resistance by others as well as yourself. Yes, you will want to go right back to the familiar. Yes, you will want to quit. However, the possibilities on the other side of your yes are far too great to allow any excuse you can come up with to stop you.

What I love most about baking is hoping it comes out right but knowing that if it doesn't I still have enough ingredients to try again. Aren't we lucky that we have such a generous God that he will allow us to start, mess up, start again, fail, fall, and start again? Do not lead an empty life when having a heaven backed guarantee of an overflowing one is within your reach. Sometimes the best thing you can do for you is burn a bridge you were never meant to cross again anyway. Always ensure that you are the best quality, freshly sifted version of yourself that you can be.

Chapter Ten

The Effects of a Soul Tie on a Shift

"You cannot rebuke a devil
that you continuously grant access
to your life."
—T.D. JAKES

A FRIEND of mine sent a sermon my way. I didn't always enjoy sermons. God and I had an understanding. I loved him and all but all the "preaching" wasn't really my thing. I was raised differently than most of my friends and we just didn't do all that "hollering and screaming" that one would find in some traditional churches. My church was quiet. I had several conversations with God but I never knew if he heard me.

It wasn't until one day I stepped out on my front porch and there was a bible with a note from my Uncle. From that day on I wondered why in the world out of all the people we had in the house he thought to give it to me. I didn't know what to do with it. I placed it on my bookshelf and didn't come back to it. I was always careful with it. I never left it out to get ruined and when Katrina hit New Orleans it was the first item I made sure I had with me. That bible has some staying power.

It wasn't until I reached a certain age that I found myself within its pages searching for the meaning to everything I had gone through, was up against, and might experience. I still couldn't figure out why he gave me that book. I asked him one day and his response was simple: **"You will need it to determine the way to go and the people to stay away from."** I thought I was already a good judge of character so I didn't think much about his statement. It wasn't until I watched and listened to the sermon my friend sent me that everything came full circle.

The sermon in its infinite beauty and its entirety discussed negative soul ties. It defined such a soul tie as a bond to someone or something that is detrimental to your growth. What is it about a soul tie that makes it harmful? The harm comes in the attachment phase. We as people of spiritual genetic makeup must understand the value and power present in our attachment. That attachment could be an addiction, a bad habit, an alternative lifestyle, or abuse. When we attach to something we are in essence saying "this is an extension of me." Just like God did with Adam in the Garden of Eden. He made him in his image and after his likeness. When he created Eve he made her from "his rib" to strengthen her attachment to Adam. Our attachments are designed to be and outward display of an inward relationship. The very thing that you are attached to has the power to either develop you or destroy you. The story of Abraham, Sarah, and Haggar is an honest account of this very thing.

Abraham and Sarah were married. Sarah had been unable to produce an heir for Abraham. Knowing that he desired a child, she made her servant Haggar available to him so that she would produce an heir for him. In the old days, it was customary for things like this to occur. However, what Sarah didn't account for was the bond that would form between Haggar and Abraham, the amount of time they would spend together or even the possible pillow talk that might occur. She didn't account for their intimacy reaching beyond the bedroom. In science, we see that atoms are strange mini particles. Individually they are small in size, but the minute they make a certain bond to another atom they become forceful, powerful, and displayed in a way that they can no longer fly under the radar and be ignored. The same was true for Haggar's growing belly. While Sarah's initial thought was to "figure out a way" to give her husband a child, she neglected to consult with God before taking action. By the time she realized what she had done, the baby was here, Abraham was happy, and Haggar was now her enemy. When Sarah became pregnant and after giving birth, the children found themselves like many siblings having a quarrel. Sarah saw it and in her rage said that both Haggar and her child had to leave her house. As one would expect, this was upsetting to Abraham as this is his seed. His son, his child. How can he put them out? Sarah did not think twice about it and so we see Haggar and her son banished.

There are a lot of life lessons to be learned from this biblical text. The one that I want to point out is how difficult it must have been for Abraham to give up his son and Haggar. How difficult it is for any of us to give up something we like, someone we love, because the bond itself is toxic and if left untreated it will kill us. The bond between the three of them was a strong one. This was his first taste at a family but his wife had spoken and it was her house as well. The soul tie between Haggar and Abraham is what aggravated Sarah the most. The bond between them. The reason I believe it upset her is because Sarah wanted that bond and didn't know she didn't have it until she saw it between the two of them.

Think for a moment. How many bonds in your life are at play right now? How many things or people are you attached to that are silent killers? The things that bind us are the things that keeps us bound. There are areas of your life screaming for revival but you won't do it because to let this "thing" go would be to live without it, to grow without it, to be a version of you without it. That is a hard pill to swallow. What is more difficult is staying at the level of your life that you have found yourself in. Taking up residence at a mountain for 30 years when you were originally only supposed to spend 5 years there. God is speaking too many of you simply whispering "let it go" and you just can't.

Letting go does not mean you will be left alone. I know that it's frustrating and that we want to hold onto these ties for far longer than we are supposed to but **there is life in letting go.** There is survival in making the decision to cut that tie, to walk away, to close that door, to stop the shame, to surrender the guilt, and to let God renew you in every aspect. "Let go and let God" is not some cute Christian cliché. It is a daily choice to let the one who has you where you are be the one to push you into the next season of your life and set your path on fire. He will do it. He can do it. But he will not show up and produce life if it is already tied to something dead. **Loosen your grip and walk in light.**

Chapter Eleven

The Value of Your Shift

I WONDER what crosses your mind as you begin to think about the word value. For me, that word is powerful. Every day, all day, we attach value to things and to people without realizing it. Some people value the moments in the morning before everyone gets up, some value the stillness of the house at night once everyone is tucked away. We value vacations, "me time," friendly outings, and family dinners. We value our time, our money, our family, our friends, our spirituality, our jobs, and our country. The thing about value is that alone it holds no power and no weight. However, the minute you attach it to something it's like a kernel of popcorn bursting from the heat and pressure. The thing you value becomes significant almost overnight. If the potential of valuing something is so important why do we place value in things that are not good, no longer good, or downright toxic for us?

There is power in your shift. There is an untapped reservoir of opportunity with your name on it but there is a requirement to access it. Remember being in high school. I know for me it wasn't as horrible as some people's experience but there were times it was unpleasant. I can remember wishing I had bigger calf muscles or wanting to have a certain hairstyle that Mama didn't approve of that all the girls seemed to be wearing at the time. No matter how much I pleaded with her she never changed her mind and I was never able to experience that type of hairstyle. Our values were different. Mama's value was in me looking my age. My value at the time was being able to have matching hairstyles for dance pictures. When there are two people each holding their value system at the highest level they ultimately find themselves on opposite ends of the value spectrum. They look for common ground but they are unable to find it. One of them esteems their value to be best.

No one on earth is more valuable than you. I'm not saying that to give you the greenlight to tell everyone in your circle how valuable you are repeatedly. I am, however, expecting you to believe that you are. Jesus Christ was sent as a sacrifice for your life. God in heaven made the entire world in seven days. You are his masterpiece. You are his greatest creation. You are the manifestation of his heart's desires and grandest thoughts. If you believe you are all of this, why then do you find yourself smack dab in the middle of life questioning the author of your life? Why is it when he has ordered your steps, made the crooked path straight, do you argue with him about you? Do you know how difficult it is to argue with God about you?

We sit and we walk through life giving God the second degree about decisions, choices, and shifts. We talk until we are blue in the face. We pray until our knees have lines on them. We cry until our eyes get puffy and swollen and then we have the audacity to ask him yet again to lead us in the right direction. If only we valued his voice more than we did our own thoughts our lives would look and feel much differently.

There have been times in your life when you know you have heard him say to do a certain something yet you stood still, moved out of line, or even disobeyed him like Jonah did running in the opposite direction. When this happens you will find yourself in such a place where you begin to question yourself, doubt your decisions, or suppress a shift for fear of being wrong. Being wrong is not a sign of failure. It is in fact a sign of strength. It is not a coincidence that we are instructed often to repent of our sins. God's grace is big enough to encompass our wrongdoings. He wants to know if we value his thoughts, his ways, his words more than we do our own. What you value grows. When you trust the shift that is taking place in your life and you trust the one that is shifting you, the possibilities become endless.

I found myself reflecting on the story of Abraham. He was told to go to a place and to leave behind everything he possessed to receive a land that God had for him. Just imagine for a moment that happening to you in your life right now.

Imagine leaving behind all of your things, some family members, and just going where you are told to go. The beauty in this story is that God did what he said he would. You can always count on him to stick to his word and to deliver on his promises. Even more beautiful was when Abraham arrived he was given land as far as he could see. He was made the father of many nations because of his obedience. You have no idea who or what is attached to your shift. There are many lives and dreams attached to your obedience. You have to go so that they can go. I know we all like being comfortable. There is nothing better than wearing comfortable clothing or shoes. No better feeling than getting home after a long day and getting into a comfortable warm bed. Even in all that comfort there are still some moments we have to be uncomfortable. You can't relax if there is laundry to be done or food to prepare. You can't relax if there are children to help or a spouse in need. You can't relax if bills are due and money is funny. The balance of life is not in the times that we are comfortable. The balance is found when we will still obey God, value his voice and submit to his presence, in the times when we are most uncomfortable.

Chapter Twelve

Recovering from a Shift

"Better an oops than a what if."

—AUTHOR UNKNOWN

RECOVERY is defined as *the ability to return to a normal state of mind, health or strength.* When you experience a life-altering moment, you begin to look at your life and your choices through a different lens. Sometimes you feel alone on your journey. Know that you are not. There is not one single person on this earth who is alone. I know that's hard to imagine. It's difficult to say that when you pass a homeless person on the street surrounded by the few belongings they possess. It's hard to comprehend when you see a child that has been put up for adoption. It's difficult to fathom when you have become the mother of a child that by society's standards does not fit the description of "normal" and you cannot call upon your friends because they do not understand your plight. It feels as though you were doing just fine in life and right when you least expected it everything stops and you have to in essence "re-calculate" to adjust for the change you didn't ask for, don't want, and have no earthly idea how you will get through it. I know that it is difficult to see but it is for your benefit that this has happened.

Shifts are not sent to disrupt your life but to develop your character. They are meant to be the water and nutrients necessary for your growth. They are the soil by which new life can be planted. Often times we view our troubles as a nuisance. They become one more thing on our already full plates. We do not believe we should have to suffer for anything yet we want everything. Suffering is a part of life. It is, in its presence, that we seek things beyond ourselves. It is during those times that we must trust our lives in the hands of someone we cannot see. Doing that is not easy. We begin to question the author of our lives and say "if you love me surely you wouldn't send this or have me go through that." The "going through" is where the work in you begins. Joseph was a slave before his story changed, because of David's sins he lost a child, Jonah disobeyed God and still had to go where he sent him, Saul did what he wanted and it cost him his kingdom, Elijah didn't think he could do what God asked of him so God replaced him and Jesus died so that we may be free. All of these are accounts of those who "suffered." Some of whom paid the ultimate price.

Shifting in all its infinite beauty is not a stronghold or a burden but a gateway to freedom. If you do not shift you will not grow into all that you were created to be. The shifting in your life is a movement to a higher level of one's self. You are being renewed, rediscovered, replanted, and restored. I have never seen a plant that grew without going through a little dirt first. The dirt is necessary for growth for without it we run the risk of being somewhere we were never meant to be. It is in the dirt that you become strengthened and refined.

After the shift is a space and time I refer to as recovery. When you recover from something it is your body's way of taking the necessary rest needed to heal, to begin anew. It is a point in time that cannot be dominated by humans. Recovery is just as powerful as the shift itself. It is necessary to the shift. While shifting you get so bogged down with the debris of change that often times you might miss out on the joy of changing. Change has always been looked at as something negative, inconvenient. Change is the only measure of success we have. Think about it. If I am driving a Toyota and 3 years later I am driving a Mercedes we can agree that something somewhere in my life changed in those 3 years. The recovery is designed to reflect on the shift. It is during this time that 3 questions ultimately come to mind:

- Who was I before this shift happened?
- How has this shift changed my life for the better? For worse?
- Who am I as a result of this shift?

The biggest biblical shift I can think of is the story of Adam and Eve. They were given a kingdom and within that kingdom, they had everything they could have ever wanted. But one wrong decision placed them on the outside. It brought things into their lives they had no knowledge of before. Their shift and recovery set the standard for all of the shifts we will experience in our lifetime.

Some of your shifts will be pleasant. Some of them will be uncomfortable, but all of them will be necessary. God always provides. Knowing this should be what you focus on in those times of impossibility. In those times where you feel you have nowhere to turn, no one to call, and everything to lose. In my life, I have never experienced a season where God did not have my back. He didn't agree with all of my decisions but just like an earthly father loves their child regardless of their behavior, he has been a constant comfort for me. He has your back too.

Pay attention to the shifts in your life. Attached to them are blessings you couldn't have imagined for yourself. Be obedient to the change and mindful of his goodness at all times. **He will never ask you to go to a place where he is not there waiting for you willing and able to restore you to a normal state of mind, health, and strength.**

Acknowledgements

I would like to acknowledge God. For without him not one word would have been typed. It is with my entire life that I serve him. Tonia Askins for the many lunch dates we spent pouring over the ideas for this book. I thank you for entrusting me with such a vision. To my family and friends your love and encouragement during this process has been instrumental in getting me to this point. Thank you. To the shift that took place within me that helped to orchestrate this publication thank you for the purging of weeds and the start of a new garden.

About the Life Shifter

Tasha T. Huston is a native New Orleanian whose writing is influenced by her love of the culture and her upbringing. You can also find bits and pieces of her experiences and self-taught lessons in her writing which she uses to let others know that they are not alone, in whatever they are going through. She was selected to be a featured writer in Writer's *Anonymous,* an online poetry publication, after submitting only one piece of her work. Her work has also appeared in *Nia Magazine,* an online publication geared toward enriching the lives of women of color. She is the author of No Chumps Allowed: *7 Keys to Activating your Inner Champion.* She holds a B.A.in Sociology from Louisiana State University and both a Bachelor's and Master's in Theology and Religious Studies. She currently works in the Social Services Industry helping families and children overcome behavioral problems. In her spare time, Huston enjoys playing with her dog, Dio, going for a run around the lake, reading, and traveling.

About The Visionary

The Freedom Teacher, **Tonia Askins,** has serviced emerging entrepreneurs, existing small business owners and corporations for over fifteen years globally. Her client list ranging from Ministers to Computer Application Developers is just as diverse as her experience. As an author and speaker her books and teachings set a tone of spiritual precedent and standard of individual ability, achievement and victorious living. Within the world of publishing she has been a forerunner and continues to trail blaze the way for countless authors through coaching and training classes.

A no limits mind-set and passion for people are her main driving force. "I fuel people to do three things: be creative, sow and grow. Be Creative about how you go about achieving your goals, sow into purposeful projects that help others and grow by continually remaining a student of life."

To learn more about services and partnership opportunities within your area you may email her personally at **tonia@toniaaskins.com** or call **1-866-5LetsGo(53-8746).** For more formation on products, feel free to visit on line, **www.toniaaskins.com.**

www.ingramcontent.com/pod-product-compliance
Lightning Source LLC
Chambersburg PA
CBHW060556100426
42742CB00013B/2586